WINNING THE HEARTS AND MINDS: THE INJUSTICE OF HUMANIZING WAR

LUIS ARTURO SUAREZ

DEDICATION

I dedicate this work to my beloved wife who would never let me quit. Without her unwavering support and belief in me this work would have never been completed. And to my dear parents for believing that I am always capable of doing more.

CONTENTS

ACKNOWLEDGMENTS

I wish to thank Ms. Jacki Collert for her support and reminding me every day not to quit on myself. Her personal experiences and insight on strategic issues was instrumental in keeping my mind fresh of ideas throughout this program. Dr. Edward J. Hagerty for his accurate advice when I needed it the most and for convincing me to give it another try. Finally, I would also like to thank Dr. Martin Catino for his outstanding dedication and valuable advice throughout the course of this work.

1 INTRODUCTION

After its remarkable victory in World War II (WWII), the United States has not been able to achieve the same level of success in any of the major conflicts it has been involved in thereafter. And although its military has evolved into the greatest military power the world has ever witnessed, it continues to struggle against much smaller and weaker adversaries. By choosing not to follow the laws created to humanize war, these types of enemies have successfully lured the United States into abandoning many of its warfare advantages while adopting doctrines that are exploitable by the insurgents they wish to defeat, creating a series of detrimental effects which this paper intends to explore.

When the United States invaded Iraq in March of 2003, the fears and uncertainties created by the terrorist attacks on September 11th of 2001 where still very fresh in the minds of the American people who appeared to be supportive of a new war. This same support was evident in congress where the authorization to conduct military operations against Iraq was passed with little resistance with the House of Representatives' voting 296 to 133[1] and the Senate totaling 77 to 33 in favor of the use of force.[2] The memories of the overwhelming victory against Saddam Hussein's forces during the Gulf War of 1991 and the ease with which the U.S. military toppled the Taliban in Afghanistan in 2001 probably did not help to envision the type of war Iraq would eventually become.

A few weeks after the United States invaded Iraq in 2003, a swift victory

---

[1] Office of the Clerk, last modified October 10, 2002, accessed August 29, 2014, http://clerk.house.gov/evs/2002/roll455.xml.
[2] United States Senate, last modified October 11, 2002, accessed August 29, 2014, http://www.senate.gov/legislative/LIS/roll_call_lists/roll_call_vote_cfm.cfm?congress=1 07&session=2&vote=00237.

1

with little casualties on both sides of the conflict appeared to come into fruition when President Bush delivered his "Mission Accomplished" speech. The ideal war, resembling the one in 1991against the same country, seemed to assure the world these types of conflicts were the new norm; little did anyone know the true war in Iraq had not even started. Soon enough the United States would find itself fighting the enemy's ideal war where the insurgents' blatant disregard for the laws of war helped them to level the battlefield against the American overwhelming firepower which became virtually irrelevant because of the their strict adherence to these laws.

This paper will analyze what impacts the rules of war had during this conflict and if the American COIN strategy had its desired effects, while hypothesizing on alternative approaches. In order to arrive to a valid answer, this research will use a combination of theories, current events, and testimonials to draw comparisons and conclusions in order to help support this paper's main purpose which is to substantiate that today's approach to war is inadequate for the type of enemy the civilized world is facing and it is actually harming the people these rules were meant to protect.

Additionally, there are many theorists who describe how history has witnessed the transformation of wars and explain the need for strong nations like the United States to adapt or completely change their conventional ways of fighting these conflicts if they wish to be successful. Apparently, the military brass has bought into these schools of thought and in some cases military officers are the ones promoting them. COIN, fourth-generation-warfare (4GW), Asymmetric warfare, and limited wars are some of the concepts utilized by the proponents of converting the United States from fighting conventionally to fighting the "new wars."

Interestingly though, all of these concepts have the common characteristic of renouncing to the need of fighting a style of total war which would obviously produce greater infrastructure destruction and loss of life. This research will explore if the different theories dedicated to the humanization of armed conflict have had any effect over the United States failing to link its political and strategic objectives with its military successes and if America's obvious diversion from exploiting the spoils of war, in an attempt to appear just and morally superior, is actually having a negative effect on America's image, its political landscape, and regional security of the battled area. Furthermore, this paper will look at the current situation in Iraq in order to deduce if the factors explained above have any correlation with the timorous American response to the current conflict it should probably feel responsible for. However, regardless of this last statement, the reality is that the current situation in Iraq delivers a supporting model of how the rules of war and the humanistic approach to these conflicts are actually limitations causing greater harm.

Finally, the laws of war designed to humanize as much as possible one of the most unfortunate and terrible events any person can experience are without a doubt well intentioned; however, the reality on the battlefield is not as simple, and to make matters worse, the unruly enemy of today has become very efficient on using these same rules as protective shields, forcing the United States to use restraint in its military capabilities and in some cases even risking its own soldiers' lives to protect others. This research will explore some of the rules that are tipping the balance in favor of the insurgents and explain how they are ironically becoming the main reason for wars to draw out longer than necessary while failing to accomplish the purposes they were created for in the first place.

Background on the Insurgency in Iraq

Because this research will use the latest war in Iraq as a basis to describe the problems created by America's acceptance to humanize war, this paper will begin by describing how the United States reverted to an old doctrine it has not been successful with in the past in order to find an exit from the asymmetric warfare Iraq had turned into. Helping to first understand how the insurgency developed in Iraq is Anthony H. Cordesman's book *Iraq's Insurgency and the Road to Civil Conflict* where he details how the United States' mishandlings during the different phases of the war in Iraq are mainly responsible for allowing the insurgents to establish themselves.[3] Cordesman, a former director of intelligence assessment in the Office of the Secretary of Defense and civilian assistant to the deputy secretary of defense, provides an outstanding chronological description of the events as they unfolded before and during the Iraq War; additionally, towards the end of the second volume, Cordesman provides a series of lessons learned and recommendations for the United States to either avoid or implement in order to prevent it from making the same mistakes made in Iraq which led to such a muddled outcome.

COIN

Also in order to cultivate a better understanding on the details and complexities of the Iraqi insurgency and how the United States dealt with it initially, this research will examine Ahmed Hashim's book *Insurgency and Counter-Insurgency in Iraq*. Hashim, a professor of Strategic Studies at the U.S. Naval War College, provides a historical perspective to the Iraq war from its beginning until the years leading to the implementation of the surge and

---

[3] Anthony H. Cordesman and Emma Davies, *Iraq's Insurgency and the Road to Civil Conflict* (Portsmouth: Greenwood Publishing Group, 2008).

General Petraeus' COIN strategy. Hashim's work explains in detail the origin and composition of the Iraqi insurgency and obviously highlights America's strategic unpreparedness and blunders for a post-war Iraq. Throughout the book, Hashim explains how the United States not only failed to prevent the outbreak of the insurgency, but also demonstrates how the U.S. military passed on the opportunity of inflicting a lethal blow to the insurgency when it had a chance because of the fear of causing too many casualties.[4] Hashim's historical facts of the Iraq war even before the implementation of Petraeus' COIN should help this paper by supporting the idea that the American way of waging war today is not the most adequate.

On this issue, Kenneth M. Pollack director of the Saban Center for Middle East Policy at the Brookings Institution, and Irena L. Sargsyan, a research analyst for the same organization, have an interesting article titled *The Other Side of the COIN: Perils of Premature Evacuation from Iraq.* Here Pollack and Sargsyan explain how COIN operations in Iraq were simply inadequate for this type of culture and one of the reasons is because COIN has the propensity of politicizing the indigenous military which is a bad recipe for newly established governments like Iraq. Most importantly, Pollack and Sargsyan make great emphasis that the key requirement for success in COIN is to maintain a strong and protracted military presence until complete stability is achieved, something the United States has failed to do in many places including Iraq.[5] Pollack and Sargsyan's main idea have relevancy to this paper because it intends to discover if one of the reasons why the United States is failing to achieve its strategic objectives is partly due to fear of appearing too imperialistic, thus allowing public opinion to drive strategy.

Obviously an important point this research paper seeks to explain is the reasons for America's struggle with defeating insurgencies. The book *Beating Goliath: Why Insurgencies Win* by Jeffrey Record, a defense policy critic with experience ranging from pacification advisor in Vietnam to legislative assistant for national security affairs in Capitol Hill and currently serving as a strategy professor in the Air Force's Air War College, focuses on non-state actors and the factors which favor the insurgency against the stronger force. This book also dives into the COIN strategy applied in Iraq and compares it to the one implemented in Vietnam; [6] while he makes it clear

---

[4] Ahmed S. Hasim, Insurgency and Counter-Insurgency in Iraq (Ithaca, NY: Cornell University Press, 2006), 36.

[5] Kenneth M. Pollack and Irena L. Sargsyan, "The Other Side of the COIN: Perils of Premature Evacuation from Iraq," Washington Quarterly 33, no. 2 (Spring 2010): 19-25, accessed August 17, 2014, DOI: 10.1080/01636601003661787.

[6] Jeffrey Record, Beating Goliath: Why Insurgencies Win (Washington, DC: Potomac Books, 2007), 68.

they are different wars and a different styles of enemy, he does expose how America's weakness is to continue to make the same mistakes and not learn from the past.[7] So although record is not a critic of COIN, he does highlight the fact that the Unites States is simply not efficient at executing this type of strategy; a hypothesis this research paper intends to explore.

Colonel Gian Gentile, an active duty Army officer is a professor of history in West Point who served as a battalion commander in Iraq. Having to endure firsthand the incongruences between COIN in theory and COIN in practice, Colonel Gentile has become an open critic of the COIN concept. In his book, *Wrong Turn: America's Deadly Embrace of Counter-Insurgency*, Gentile writes about his experiences in Iraq, but he also focuses on the direction the war in Afghanistan is taking; he explains facts such as how COIN was already being conducted by American forces before Petraeus and his FM 3-24 became known as the saviors of the Iraq War;[8] and dedicates an entire chapter on the British COIN campaign in Malaya in order to clarify how American strategist have missed the importance of the use of force as a critical part of its success.[9] Clearly, Gentile's main focus in his book is to remind the reader that COIN is a flawed concept that is convenient for politicians, but not for winning wars.

In order to expose the effects of COIN over the servicemen implementing it on the battlefield, this research paper will have to review the doctrinal publication where these principles have been introduced. Generals Petraeus and Amos' *The United States Army and the United States Marine Corps Counterinsurgency Field Manual* undoubtedly provides the necessary insight of the COIN strategy to be able to extrapolate how it supposedly changed the direction the war in Iraq was taking before General Petraeus taking charge of this theater of operations. By comparing what is imparted in this publication with its detractors point of view and the testimonials of those who lived it on the ground, this paper intends to make the case that many of the principles imposed by the COIN doctrine are not congruent with the nature of war, are responsible for placing American servicemen and women in danger, and have failed to deliver anything which resembles victory for America.

Restraint and Limited Wars

Patricia Sullivan, an Associate Professor at University of North Carolina, wrote an article published by the Journal of Conflict Resolution titled *War Aims and War Outcomes: Why Powerful State Lose Limited Wars*, in this article,

---

[7] Ibid, 104.
[8] Gian P. Gentile, Wrong Turn: America's Deadly Embrace of Counterinsurgency (New York: New Press, 2013), 93.
[9] Ibid, 48.

Sullivan proposes that stronger nations mainly fail against weaker forces because although the more powerful nations have all of the equipment, forces, and finances; it is the weaker force who holds the greatest resolve and is willing to risk more than the stronger nation. Sullivan's article hits right at the center of this paper's argument that the United States is only hurting itself by limiting its military superiority and being too fearful for the loss of life on either side of the spectrum.[10] Consistent with this ideology is Dr. Zhivan Alach's article published by SSI and titled *The New Aztecs: Ritual and Restraint in Contemporary Western Military Operations*; a former analyst for the New Zealand Defense Force and a Ph.D. in defense policy, Alach perfectly describes why Western nations have drifted away from the teachings of Clausewitz and are now resembling the Aztec empire of 500 years ago, emphasizing how the Aztecs chose not to kill their enemies and even adapted their weapons so that their enemies would survive to be used for religious purposes later.[11] Throughout the article, Alach uses historical examples where the United States has limited its military powers and has obviously suffered the consequences for doing so.

The theory of different types of war is controversial and one which is rightly and fortunately being resisted by a sector in the strategic circles. Because this research paper seeks to make a connection between the humanization of the U.S. military and the ideological influence pacifists have had over the American approach to war, it is important to study the proponents of new wars and the need to transform the military into a humanitarian force for making friends rather than destroying enemies. The book *New Wars* by Herfried Munkler, a professor of political Science at the University of Humboldt in Berlin, argues how war has changed because nation-states have giving up its exclusivity and now non-state actors have taken up the role of waging wars. Munkler, however, does explain how this phenomenon is actually a return to what Europe looked like prior to the end of the Thirty Year War.[12] Throughout his work, Munkler analyzes war theorists such as Clausewitz and Martin van Creveld to cover both sides of the spectrum and provide the reader with a choice to which theory makes most sense.

An interesting article which provides an opposite point of view to Munkler's book is presented by Bart Schuurman, a researcher at Leiden University's Centre for Terrorism and Counterterrorism in The Hague, Netherlands. In his article titled *Clausewitz and the "New Wars" Scholars* and published in the journal Parameters, Schuurman counters the ideology

---

[10] Patricia L. Sullivan, "War Aims and War Outcomes: Why Powerful States Lose Limited Wars," *Journal of Conflict Resolution* 51, no. 3 (June 2007)

[11] Zhivan Alach, "The New Aztecs: Ritual and Restraint in Contemporary Western Military Operations," last modified July 2011, 1-2, PDF.

[12] Herfried Munkler, The New Wars (Oxford: Polity, 2005), 42.

behind the school of thought which describes today's conflicts as a new style of warfare that requires a departure from Clausewitz' principles on war and an adaptation on behalf of the greater powers to fight another form of war.[13] In his article, Schuurman does a good job at utilizing a variety of 'New Wars' scholars' arguments to make the point on how they are only blurring the concept and true purpose of and for war. Schuurman's article presents a point of view which clearly defends Clausewitz' trinity of war and how, if interpreted correctly, it still has applicability for the wars the United States is facing today. Schuurman is a evidently a believer that the new wars concepts are distracting the great powers like the United States from achieving its strategic objectives against much smaller and weaker opponents.

Also, Antulio Echevarria, the Director of National Security Affairs and Acting Chairman of the Regional Strategy and Planning Department at the Strategic Studies Institute (SSI), has an article posted by SSI titled *Fourth-Generation War and Other Myths* where he completely debunks the theory behind the evolvement of war by explaining how today's wars, including the war on terrorism, have the same essence than past wars. Also, Echevarria clearly defends Clausewitz' trinity of war by attacking the 4GW theorists' poor historical facts and lack of originality in their ideas.[14] Throughout the article, Echevarria also offers many historical passages which should help counterbalance the choice of COIN and other humanitarian concepts affecting America's new approach to war and he clearly defends the true purpose of the military institution, which is to fight wars.

Morality and the Just War Theory

In order to support this paper's main idea about America's humanization of war, it is important to analyze the many theories that might have been an influential factor for the strongest military nation in the world to take such direction. Brian Orend, a Director of International Studies and philosophy professor at the University of Waterloo, has written multiple books related to human rights and international justice and in this paper his book, *The Morality of War*, provides an analytical approach to three different schools of thought related to this precise topic. Orend's book offers a profound background of the Just War Theory, its origins, and its applications through a historical perspective.[15] Then, he uses the last two sections of the book to analyze the pacifists and realists approaches and

---

[13] Bart Schurman, "Clausewitz and the 'New Wars' Scholars," Parameters, Spring 2010, 95.

[14] Antulio J. Echevarria, "Fourth-Generation War and Other Myths," last modified November 2005, 6. PDF.

[15] Brian Orend, The Morality of War (Peterborough, Ont.: Broadview Press, 2006), 4.

how they relate to the just war theory.[16] Although Orend is a supporter of the this theory, he does deliver an unbiased examination of three different views on war which provides plenty of literature to support this paper's points and good information to help reach an accurate conclusion.

A paper analyzing and discussing just war theory would be incomplete if the work of the prominent but controversial Dr. Michael Walzer was not included. Walzer, an intellectual and political thinker, has produced a myriad of books and articles focused on the just war theory and could probably be credited for being one of the biggest contributors to America's embracement of a humanistic approach to war. Although many of Walzer's ideas are hard to agree with and are obviously biased towards pacifism, this research paper will use many of these in both ways, to agree and to contradict with; as in his article, *Coda: Can the Good Guys Win?*, where he goes from the non-sense side of the spectrum when he states soldiers' lives are pretty much irrelevant because it is more important to successfully win the hearts and minds of the occupied;[17] but then he explains how today's U.S. military leadership truly believes present wars can be won by fighting by the rules and can be lost if not.[18] An honest and probably true statement this research paper intends to debate. Other piece written by Walzer, such as *The Triumph of Just War Theory (and Dangers of Success)* will be examined during this research in order to find both, consistencies and inconsistencies, with this very important theorist's point of view and accept or contend his proposals.

The article titled *Irregular Enemies and the Essence of Strategy: Can the American Way of War Adapt?* injects a refreshing dose of common sense into the debate about America's strategic future and concept of war. The article written by Colin S. Gray, a Professor of International Politics and Strategic Studies at the University of Reading, England who served on President Reagan's General Advisory Committee on Arms Control and Disarmament, not only criticizes the multiple variants of war American Strategists have promoted, but he also breaks down how the United States does not have a clear strategy to win wars even though they succeed tactically.[19] Gray also uses many historical facts from Vietnam and Iraq to convince the reader of the incompatibility of the American military with COIN and that the concept of war must not be misconstrued so wars can be fought as such in order to achieve the nation's strategic objectives above all.[20] Lastly, Gray's

---

[16] Ibid, 5

[17] Michael Walzer, "Coda: Can the Good Guys Win?," The European Journal of International Law 24, no. 1 (2013): 443.

[18] Ibid.

[19] Colin S. Gray, "Enemies and the Essence of Strategy: Can the American Way of War Adapt?," March 2006, 4-5. PDF.

[20] Ibid, 9-11.

article provides a brutal but much needed honesty which this research paper will benefit from, as should the leadership of this great nation.

Testimonials

Finally, aside from theories and the hypothesis raised by scholars, this research paper will need to draw information from those who have lived these strategies and concepts on the ground and not just through second and third hand reports. As with Colonel Gentile explained earlier, this research will also examine retired Colonel Bing West's contributions to COIN from his firsthand experiences in Vietnam, Afghanistan, and Iraq. Even though, Bing West is a proponent of COIN, it is important to notice his experiences with the Combined Action Platoon (CAP) in Vietnam are very different from the apache type forts implemented in Iraq. Also, throughout Bing West's book *No True Glory: A Frontline Account of the Battle for Fallujah*, the reader can find the struggles and dangers American servicemen have had to endure due to the restrictions imposed on them by the rules of war and the COIN strategy.[21] Adding to this type of real-life literature is the book *Nightcap at Dawn: American Soldiers' Counterinsurgency in Iraq* by J.B. Walker, a collective pen consisting of former Army soldiers who were part of the COIN campaign in Iraq and where it clearly describes the frustrations caused by following rules of engagement (ROEs) which drove their morale to dangerous levels.[22]

Summary and Conclusions

The intent of this research paper is to be as impartial as possible by using literature from opposing schools of thought in regards to the conduct of war and therefore be able to provide contrasting arguments required to reach an honest and balanced response. So far, the research conducted has been able to establish two sides of the argument. On one side of the discussion are those theorists and subject matter experts who promote law of war, the Just War Theory, and the effectiveness of winning the hearts and minds as a strategy for war; while on the other side of the aisle are those who question the validity or effectiveness of some of these proposals and conversely have more of a Clausewitzian ideology towards war. And even though, the conducted research has encountered a disproportion in the literature that favors theorists for a just and humane style of warfare, the material dedicated to protect and defend the true nature of war

---

[21] Bing West, *No True Glory: A Frontline Account of the Battle for Fallujah*, paperback ed. (New York: Bantam Books, 2006).
[22] J. B. Walker, *Nightcap at Dawn: American Soldiers' Counterinsurgency in Iraq* (New York: Skyhorse Pub., 2012).

effectively demystifies the pacifist attempt to placate the strongest military in the world.

This research has encountered a well-defined line separating on one side philosophers and strategists who promote the barbaric nature of war as a thing of the past with no place within civilized nations like the United States and its allies, with the theorists on the other end of the spectrum which are attempting to prevent the military from becoming distracted from their true mission and innate character. Unfortunately, based on the historical evidence, it does appear the American leadership has accepted the idea that war has changed and therefore they have become obsessed with trying to transform the approach to how it must be fought, choosing to abandon the style of warfare the United States is actually suited for, while opting to fight wars in a way that is consistent with the effort of humanizing war.

From Vietnam to Iraq and Afghanistan, the United States has obviously failed to produce the same effects achieved during WWII and even though history and current events demonstrate how America continues to come out empty handed when choosing to limit its military power to satisfy popular concepts like the just war theory and the rules established by the international laws of war, the United States still appears to be blinded by the attractive ideology of holding the moral high-ground even if it represents defeat.

This paper seeks to establish a correlation between the emergence of theories and concepts such as the New Wars theories, Just War Theorists, and COIN with the political urgency to create a style of warfare that is least rejected by public opinion. Also, this paper attempts to demonstrate how pacifists have successfully affected political and military leadership to believe wars are best fought as humane as possible and that the only way to defeat an insurgency, the enemy of today, is to renounce to the conventional methods that have ironically worked for America in the past, but are easily being portrayed as inhumane and almost barbaric. In order to counter this type of ideology, this research paper will use the arguments and theories defending the nature of war as an unchanged act, and make the case of how America's awesome military power must be utilized to its full capacity regardless of the type of enemy.

The combination of these publications should deliver the desired framework which will help corroborate this paper's basic assumptions about the inadequacy of the rules of war for today's conflicts and how they are causing more harm than good by limiting military powers like the United States from quickly and effectively defeating these smaller and weaker forces, mainly due to them being allowed to hide behind the innocent people the humanitarian rules and laws are meant to protect. This paper will also attempt to explain how the more humanitarian approach is at fault for protracting conflicts, hence, creating a series of effects which only benefit the insurgents who understand how Americas' will and support for war eventually dwindles with time, leading to a hasty withdraw which will leave the door open for those who have no regards for human rights to immediately fill in the vacuum produced upon the strong nation's departure; an effective game insurgencies fighting the United States have learned to play all too well.

2 THE BIRTH OF THE INSURGENCY IN IRAQ

According to Anthony Cordesman, the idea that the Iraqi people would see American forces as liberators and immediately embrace democracy was a great miscalculation on behalf of the Bush administration.[23] In fact, it is the total removal of Saddam Hussein's regime that is credited for the state of chaos and anarchy that lead to the development of an insurgency which would embroil the American military in a war they were not prepared for; as described in an article titled, *Forging a Key, Turning a Lock: Counterinsurgency Theory in Iraq 2006-2008* by Lydia Walker, who is currently a PhD candidate at Harvard in International History and a former a nuclear policy and scenario researcher for the Institute of Peace and Conflict Studies and the Hertog Global Strategy Initiative:

> By June 2003 central Iraq was in the midst of a low-level, decentralized insurgency, a state of affairs acknowledged by U.S. officials and senior military officers. By the following year, the ongoing conflicts in Afghanistan and Iraq convinced Army leadership that new counterinsurgency doctrine was needed. Over the next two years and through much debate, the U.S. military carried out the process of rethinking COIN doctrine in order to make it a viable tool for present conflicts and to examine its theoretical underpinnings for future applicability.[24]

---

[23] Anthony H. Cordesman and Emma Davies, Iraq's Insurgency and the Road to Civil Conflict (Portsmouth: Greenwood Publishing Group, 2008), 6.

[24] Lydia Walker, "Forging a Key, Turning a Lock: Counterinsurgency Theory in Iraq 2006-2008," Studies in Conflict & Terrorism 32, no. 10 (October 2009): 911, accessed August 17, 2014, DOI:10.1080/10576100903185586.

Nevertheless, the complete removal of the Hussein regime was only one of many factors that facilitated the formation of the insurgency style warfare the United States allowed itself to get into. According to Anthony Cordesman, one of the failures committed by the United States was the overestimation of how much international support America would receive, especially from its own allies.[25]

Because the international community, represented in the United Nations (UN), has become so attached to the sovereignty of its members and learned to be conveniently selective in the utilization of force, the United States and its few unwavering allies were left alone to clean up their own mess. Also, because the American coalition had used the presence of weapons of mass destruction (WMD) as the main pretext to invade Iraq and the fact that these weapons were never found made this war ever more unpopular and lacking validation.[26] And although the American forces had little problems defeating the Iraqi army and establishing themselves as the presumptive victors, the United States had failed miserably at taking true control over a nation now immersed in chaos and anarchy.

The United States should have expected for a guerrilla force to develop even before the invasion was conducted, but obviously failed to plan accordingly and instead went into Iraq with the plans to withdraw even before stabilization had been achieved; as explained by Cordesman, the U.S. military intended to conduct major troop reductions just a few months after the removal of Hussein's power.[27] This lack of commitment was evident with the deficiency in coalition numbers and equipment required to control critical areas in Iraq, a gap exploited by the anarchist; as described by Cordesman, "The inability to secure key centers of gravity and rear areas helped create a process of looting that effectively destroyed the existing structure of governance and security."[28] A timid approach on behalf of the most powerful nation in the world because of its refusal to carry out a total war concept and instead insisting on using limited war for every conflict, a concept which will be discussed further in this paper.

Because of America's preference for limited warfare, which facilitate the respect of the rules of war, and its good intentions to avoid collateral damages during the invasion, there were a countless amount of weapons left over from Hussein's regime to be utilized by a great amount of former military and militias who simply hid amongst the population during America's strongest moment.[29] This combination of mistakes made by the

---

[25] Anthony H. Cordesman and Emma Davies, Iraq's Insurgency and the Road to Civil Conflict (Portsmouth: Greenwood Publishing Group, 2008), 9.

[26] Ibid, 15.

[27] Ibid, 10.

[28] Ibid.

[29] Ibid, 13-14

United States had unfortunately created the perfect environment for an insurgency to develop; and once Hussein's regime was not there to crush any type uprising, the Sunni clerics and leadership, who during Saddam Hussein's reign had resisted him the most and even attempted to overthrow him, enjoyed more freedom to rally their base, but now their rhetoric was now directed against the American coalition.[30]

Although the Sunnis failed to create national unity to seize political control over the government, they were able generate enough influence throughout the area known as the Sunni Triangle where a Sunni stronghold called Fallujah, was the most affected by the American rigidity which destroyed their methods of commercial subsistence because they were considered illegal by the American standards; and also because a great number of their men belonged to the Iraqi military, which happened to be misguidedly disbanded by the coalition in the Summer of 2003.[31] The Iraqi resistance was now in motion and the United States was, unknowingly and unprepared, facing an insurgency; as described by Ahmed Hashim, "...top Bush administration officials acknowledged in late summer 2003 that their plans for post war Iraq had been flawed on the security front. They admitted that little thought was given to the possibility of resistance."[32]

The last time the United States had to fight an insurgency or a guerrilla type warfare was during the Vietnam War, an unfortunate event in America's history the government and military leadership did not want the public opinion to remember; and although their pushback was correct to not compare Vietnam with Iraq, it was naïve not to accept the United States was fighting a new type of insurgency.[33] An insurgency which could have been devastated in April of 2004 when the US military went on the offensive in Fallujah; unfortunately, the new U.S. military school of thought prevented this from happening and instead worked out a cease fire with the insurgents who obviously saw the American timorous attitude as a tremendous political and even a military victory because they were still able to continue to fight at a later date.[34]

The unfortunate view of the Americans in Fallujah was to believe they were in a no-win situation because they feared the loss of life would have had the same negative effect as defeat;[35] an obvious and troubling sign that the United States was a military beast which could be manipulated and held back by exploiting its adherence to the rules of war and unwillingness to

---

[30] Ahmed S. Hasim, Insurgency and Counter-Insurgency in Iraq (Ithaca, NY: Cornell University Press, 2006), 21-23.

[31] Ibid, 25-27.

[32] Ibid, 29-30.

[33] Ibid, 30.

[34] Ibid, 36-37.

[35] Ibid.

accept loss of life on either side of the conflict. The American strategy for the rest of the war was not innovative at all and had been tried before during the war no one wanted to remember.

3 COIN IN IRAQ

Predictably, the United States reverted to the old tactics of COIN and kept forcing it as a strategy to win these wars, but Jeffry Record describes COIN as a strategy that is primarily focused on winning the trust of the local population rather than destroying the enemy and contains many factors Americans were not prepared for during the Iraq War, more troops and a lot a of patience.[36]

After three years of little progress for the Americans and the opposite for the insurgency, the United States implemented what came to be known as the "Surge" led by the author of the Army's new counterinsurgency manual, General David Petraeus. In his manual, FM 3-24, there is an interesting section titled "Paradoxes of counterinsurgency operations" where it urges commanders to adopt a mentality not consistent with the warrior attitude most military men, especially infantrymen, usually are trained to have. For example, FM 3-24 explains:

1. Sometimes, the More You Protect Your Force, the Less Secure You May Be.
2. Sometimes, the More Force Is Used, the Less Effective It Is.
3. The More Successful the Counterinsurgency Is, the Less Force Can Be Used and the More Risk Must Be Accepted.
4. Sometimes Doing Nothing Is the Best Reaction.
5. Some of the Best Weapons for Counterinsurgency Do Not Shoot.
6. The Host Nation Doing Something Tolerably is Normally Better that Us doing It Well.
7. If a Tactic Works this Week, It Might Not Work Next Week; If it

---

[36] Jeffrey Record, Beating Goliath: Why Insurgencies Win (Washington, DC: Potomac Books, 2007), 81.

Works in this Province, It Might Not Work in the Next.
8. Tactical Success Guarantees Nothing.
9. Many Important Decisions Are Not Made by Generals.[37]

Although in the FM 3-14 literature these points are all backed up by common sense explanations for a doctrine which is centered on the ideology of winning the hearts and minds of the local populace; according to Colonel Gian Gentile, FM 3-24 is based, and almost a carbon copy, of the works of the French army Officer David Galula who wrote about his own practices when dealing with the insurgency in Algeria during the 1950's. Regrettably, this might not have been the best choice to follow as explained by Colonel Gentile himself:

But recent scholarship has shown that what Galula said worked for him in Algeria actually did not. Moreover, there is the broader question why a group of American army officers, retired and active, along with civilian intellectuals, would use French COIN tactics in Algeria as the basis of army doctrine when the French in the end lost that war.[38]

Nevertheless, the situation in Iraq after the surge did change for the best and the intensity of insurgents' attacks started to decline, bringing up the question of, did COIN succeed in Iraq? A question with a much divided answer; for example, Colonel Gentile argues:

The reasons for the drop in violence were complex: the spread of the Anbar Awakening (a revolt against al Qaeda in Iraq by Sunni tribes in western Iraq) and the co-opting of Sunni insurgents in Baghdad and other parts of Iraq; the decision by Shia militia leaders to halt their deadly campaign of slaughter against Sunni civilians; and the fact that Baghdad had become sectarian, separated into a Shia-dominated city with small enclaves of Sunnis. To be sure, the extra surge brigades played a role in the reduction of violence, but largely in their ability to reduce al Qaeda's numbers and strength through combat actions.[39]

While authors like Kenneth M. Pollack and Irena L. Sargsyan, in their article titled *The Other Side of the COIN: Perils of Premature Evacuation from Iraq* do not really question COIN's success in Iraq, they do express an issue with

---

[37] David H. Petraeus and James F. Amos, The United States Army and the United States Marine Corps Counterinsurgency Field Manual (Kissimmee, FL: Signalman Publishing, 2006), 1-28 - 1-30.
[38] Gian P. Gentile, Wrong Turn: America's Deadly Embrace of Counterinsurgency (New York: New Press, 2013), 26.
[39] Ibid, 28.

the hasty departure of the U.S. military from this country; and by using historic examples, they demonstrate how COIN operations usually work until the strong nation withdraws.[40] Furthermore, Pollack and Sargsyan's argument should also raise the question if the insurgency smartly waited out the Americans after in 2008 President Obama announced the total withdrawal of American forces from Iraq by 2010.

Another author who is cautious about writing a final chapter on Iraq and the American success is Anthony Cordesman as he wrote:

> No one can predict the outcome of Iraq's insurgency and civil conflicts. There are no direct historical models to draw upon, and there are many different paths Iraq can take. If history does provide insights, is that complex insurgencies and civil conflicts have often played out over periods of a decade or more. History also shows that even when security and stability do seem to have emerged, past sectarian and ethnic conflicts often reoccur when new factors revive past divisions and tensions.[41]

And as this paper will explain later, this would end up being exactly the case in Iraq where current events will help demonstrate the poor results originating from COIN as a strategy for truly beating an insurgency.

On this, Cordesman explains that in order to achieve success against an insurgency it is necessary to eliminate the reasons for joining the insurgency, prevent the support from the locals, and attract the active insurgence to give up arms and become part of their society.[42] Cordesman refers to this as "draining the swamp," which he suggests the United States failed to accomplish due to a number of factors which makes the American culture and mindset incompatible with this type of nation building approach.[43] He is not, however, inferring the United States is not capable of conducting these types of operations, only that the Americans have failed to do their homework before taking up the task; while highlighting the fact that sometimes draining the swamp may not be possible and leaving without achieving the objective is also an acceptable option;[44] an option taken by the Obama administration which would consequentially create a greater regional threat and a huge humanitarian catastrophe.

---

[40] Kenneth M. Pollack and Irena L. Sargsyan, "The Other Side of the COIN: Perils of Premature Evacuation from Iraq," Washington Quarterly 33, no. 2 (Spring 2010), accessed August 17, 2014, DOI: 10.1080/01636601003661787.

[41] Anthony H. Cordesman and Emma Davies, Iraq's Insurgency and the Road to Civil Conflict (Portsmouth: Greenwood Publishing Group, 2008), 730.

[42] Ibid, 734.

[43] Ibid, 734-735.

[44] Ibid, 736-737.

The decision made by President Obama to telegraph the departure of all combat forces from Iraq makes it very difficult to determine exactly the effectiveness of the COIN implemented there; however, by taking a look at what is currently taking place in Iraq it is safe to deduce the Iraqi Security Forces (ISF) and the democratically elected government were simply not prepared for the Americans to leave. The Sunni Arabs who fought against the American occupation and whose hearts and minds appear to be untouched by the coalition's COIN effort made a tremendous comeback and are now in control of a vast amount of territory between Syria and Iraq, including cities at the center of the American led COIN like Ramadi and Fallujah among others.[45]

The celebrations of the end of the war in Iraq and the cheers for no more loss of life because of the American presence there must now be quenched because the vacuum created by the United States' haste departure from the region is directly responsible for the humanitarian catastrophe taking place today in Iraq. Just a few years after the last of the American combat troops left Iraq, millions of people have been displaced from their homes, oil refineries have been seized, and a Caliphate in the now Islamic State controlled area has been declared.[46] And it is precisely the former Baathist military leadership and the thousands of insurgents who waited patiently for the American withdraw that are now liberally committing atrocities.[47]

So, as it is the case with many military strategies throughout history, only time can tell if it was effective or not; however, when crimes against humanity are being carried out upon the same people the United States spent so much blood and treasure on winning their hearts and minds by fighting as justly, humanly, and civilized as possible, then the effects are already being observed, and in this case, suffered by millions.

---

[45] Dan Murphy, "Briefing: What is the Islamic State in Iraq and the Levant (ISIS)?," The Christian Science Monitor, last modified June 23, 2014, accessed September 2, 2014, http://www.csmonitor.com/World/Middle-East/2014/0623/Briefing-What-is-the-Islamic-State-In-Iraq-and-the-Levant-ISIS.

[46] "The Iraq-ISIS Conflict in Maps, Photos and Video." The New York Times. Last modified August 20, 2014. Accessed September 2, 2014. http://www.nytimes.com/interactive/2014/06/12/world/middleeast/the-iraq-isis-conflict-in-maps-photos-and-video.html?_r=0.

[47] Dan Murphy, "Briefing: What is the Islamic State in Iraq and the Levant (ISIS)?," The Christian Science Monitor, last modified June 23, 2014, accessed September 2, 2014, http://www.csmonitor.com/World/Middle-East/2014/0623/Briefing-What-is-the-Islamic-State-In-Iraq-and-the-Levant-ISIS.

4 HAS WAR REALLY CHANGED?

While the American policymakers and its own military become more obsessed with holding the moral high-ground by creating new concepts and theories which help prevent collateral damage by attempting to humanize the American warfighter and limiting the use of America's advantages in waging war, it does appear as if the intentions to save lives and prevent indiscriminate devastation might be having the opposite effect. The intention here is not to say the American soldier must act in a barbaric way and lower him/herself to the level of the insurgent, but this paper is focused on making the point that once a nation makes the ultimate decision to go to war, it must do so with total conviction to beat the enemy into submission or until he is completely annihilated; and if the enemy adopts tactics designed to exploit the laws of war to their benefit by successful tying the hands of the law-abiding force, then there is something wrong with the rules. Nevertheless, it is important to understand these new wars concepts in order to correctly assess their influence over America's way of fighting today's wars.

Although COIN is not a new concept, it does appear this tactic has become the current choice because insurgencies are the type of enemy the United States is currently facing; therefore, it is presumed COIN is the only answer to dealing with them. However, it is important to look into COIN as a strategy and what are the true intentions for fighting this way. For example, Lieutenant Commander Frank Ledwidge, a former British Naval military intelligence officer who commanded British and multi-national units in Iraq, provides an honest assessment of his first-hand experience of dealing with COIN. In his book, *Losing Small Wars: British Military Failure in Iraq and Afghanistan*, Ledwidge quotes Admiral Boyce, a former chief of the British defense staff, while complaining to the House of Lords for the legal pressures British soldiers were enduring because of COIN, "They are being pushed in the direction in which an order could be seen as improper or legally sound...They are being pushed by people not schooled in operations but only in political correctness."[48]

A candid observation of a dangerous reality which is taking over military leaders who faithfully execute the orders given by their civilian masters who usually make decisions based on popular support at the polls rather than the world's realities, especially at war. Ledwidge also explains how COIN concepts such as "Sometimes Doing Nothing Is the Best Reaction and/or Some of the Best Weapons for Counterinsurgency Do Not Shoot" are totally opposite to what young men join the military to do and have a negative effect on not only their morale, but also on the warrior mindset soldiers should innately have during war, consequently placing servicemen and women at a conundrum of being killed in the battlefield or going to jail at home.[49]

But why COIN? Why a strong military nation like the United States is giving up on their traditional way of waging war? The answer to these questions are at the center of this paper's hypothesis, the rules of war are winning the war on war. The preoccupation for respecting human life and avoid unnecessary destruction is backfiring on the nations which supported, or even promoted, the establishment of these rules. And now that they are facing an enemy who knows how to hide behind these humanitarian guidelines the stronger nations are resorting to the not so innovative COIN tactic because of its people-centered characteristic which fits perfectly and conveniently into the rhetoric of humanizing war.

As explained by Colonel Gentile, "The myth that COIN works is catnip for advocates of US intervention overseas because it promises the possibility of successful 'better wars.'"[50] The truth is, the language found in academia and publications promoting morality of war, Just War, human rights, humanization of the battlefield, etc. appeared to have had great success in influencing the minds of the American people, policymakers, and even military leaders; and COIN provides them that comfort of holding the moral high-ground representative of a civilized world.

Ironically, the same rules that are meant to protect civilian lives, cultural infrastructures, and even the soldiers involved, are actually creating detrimental effects across the spectrum of conflict, except for the insurgents creating indiscriminate death and destruction along their path while hiding behind them. For instance, Colonel Gentile describes an anecdote of a soldier's honest assessment on how the restraints of fighting

---

[48] Frank Ledwidge, Losing Small Wars. British Military Failure in Iraq and Afghanistan (New Haven: Yale University Press, 2011), 175.

[49] Ibid, 180-181.

[50] Gian P. Gentile, Wrong Turn: America's Deadly Embrace of Counterinsurgency (New York: New Press, 2013), 139.

under the doctrine of COIN was actually making the Taliban stronger in Afghanistan because they were simply not being killed by hiding amongst the population COIN seeks to protect.[51]

This soldier's small voice brings up great similarities with the case of Fallujah explained earlier, a city which is now being victimized under the total control of the Islamist extremist who survived an American onslaught by hiding and waiting for the right time to resurface.[52] Colonel Gentile also explains how the case of the British in Malaya is used as an example of COIN success, but Gentile's historic description of the methods utilized then paints a very different picture from what has been tried to be implemented in Iraq. Gentile describes how the British created camps to separate the people from the insurgency while the British, imbedded with the Malayan police, and went out to search and destroy the insurgency; also, gentile mentions the British had to do this for a long period of time.[53]

Probably one of the main problems with COIN in Iraq was that it was a tactic implemented as a strategy and it was applied throughout the entire spectrum; a basic error explained by Colin S. Gray, "Specifically, irregular enemies and irregular forms of warfare do not, and can never, present us with a single challenge that calls for a single master doctrinal response."[54] The United States left itself out of options to deal with the insurgency and became obsessed once again with the term winning the hearts and minds, and COIN is not the answer for every irregular enemy.[55] And although in some cases COIN might have its benefits, the United States must be ready and willing to fight and destroy an irregular enemy with the same force and devastation as it would a conventional foe; as explained by Gray:

> But in wars of all kinds, warfare, bluntly stated, fighting, occurs in the context of the whole war, and it needs to be conducted in such a way that it fits the character of the war and thereby yields useful strategic effectiveness.[56]

On this issue, Kenneth M. Pollack and Irena L. Sargsyan explain how COIN operations in Iraq were simply inadequate for this type of culture and one of the reasons is because one of the key requirement for success in

---

[51] Ibid, 141.

[52] *Al-Qaeda's Resurgence in Iraq: A Threat to U.S. Interests: Hearings Before the Committee on Foreign Affairs* (2014) (statement of Mr. Brett McGurk).

[53] Gian P. Gentile, Wrong Turn: America's Deadly Embrace of Counterinsurgency (New York: New Press, 2013), 48-49

[54] Colin S. Gray, "Enemies and the Essence of Strategy: Can the American Way of War Adapt?," March 2006, 9. PDF.

[55] Ibid, 10

[56] Ibid, 11.

COIN is to maintain a strong and protracted military presence until complete stability is achieved, something the United States has failed to do in many places including Iraq.[57]

To support this critical point, Pollack and Sargsyan provide examples of countries, like Nicaragua, where the United States implemented a version of COIN and produced the same unrewarding results partly because of the same mistakes being committed today. Pollack and Sargsyan's article comparison between Iraq and how the United States intervened in Nicaragua's civil war in the 1920's is perfectly encapsulated when they stated, "Unfortunately, neither the American's nor the Nicaraguans had fully resolved the underlying problems that had led to the conflict in the first place. As a result, only months after the Marines departed, the civil war resumed, fiercer than ever…"[58] Undeniably, this is a troubling mirror image of what is taking place in Iraq today and one which Pollack and Sargsyan prophetically warned in their article written four years ago, "…unless large numbers of the departing great power's combat troops remain behind for years or decades, the United States may be committing déjà vu all over again in Iraq."[59]

Nevertheless, it is important to note the fixation with COIN as a strategy is in reality only one of the reasons why the United States is failing to achieve its strategic objectives during war. The odd concept of limited wars is without a doubt one of the models which satisfies the pacifist ideology because it at least restrains strong militaries from employing a total war approach, consequently making victory more challenging. Regrettably, it appears this has become another of the poor choices made by America's leadership as evidenced in their approach to every conflict after WWII.

In her article Patricia Sullivan describes the multiple factors and assets which make the strong nation superior than the weaker force and highlights the fact that limited wars are a bad strategy which cause stronger nations to lose against a smaller enemy, but Sullivan also explains that theorists are not able to point out why exactly do stronger nations make poor strategic decisions.[60] One of the theories which she expands upon is on the stronger nation use of limited wars and how one of the dangers for powerful nations engaging in this style of warfare is the fact they are not as committed as is the weaker side.[61] Sullivan explains this lack of commitment as mainly

---

[57] Kenneth M. Pollack and Irena L. Sargsyan, "The Other Side of the COIN: Perils of Premature Evacuation from Iraq," Washington Quarterly 33, no. 2 (Spring 2010): 19-25, accessed August 17, 2014, DOI: 10.1080/01636601003661787.

[58] Ibid, 24

[59] Ibid, 17.

[60] Patricia L. Sullivan, "War Aims and War Outcomes: Why Powerful States Lose Limited Wars," Journal of Conflict Resolution 51, no. 3 (June 2007): 497.

[61] Ibid, 499-500.

originating from the stronger nation's unwillingness to tolerate the loss of life on both sides of the conflict.[62] Simply put, countries like the United States have lost their intestinal fortitude to engage in total wars.

Also, in her article, Sullivan describes how because weaker forces understand the imbalance of force and materiel is not on their favor, it is necessary for them to risk more.[63] Yet, even though the weaker clearly understands it cannot achieve a military victory, it knows the stronger nation will erode politically as the conflict protracts.[64] And this is an undeniable fact because it has been the common characteristic in America's major wars after WWII, including Korea, Vietnam, Iraq, and potentially Afghanistan as well. All wars where the most powerful nation in the world decided to limit itself by carrying out campaigns which looked more to contain the enemy rather than destroy it.

Dr. Zhivan Alach's description of the Aztec choice of warfare is amazingly similar to what strong nations like the United States are doing today:

> The Aztecs' purpose, however, was not the conquest of their enemy, the expansion of Aztec territory, or some other goal we might term policy today; rather, it was the taking of captives for religious rituals. Restraint was key; killing a foe in battle was of little use. Thus their weapons were designed to cripple, not kill, and in battle, Aztec warriors would deliberately avoid lethal blows, thus putting themselves in danger when fighting enemies whose lives would later be forfeit and who fought to kill.[65]

Furthermore, Alach compares the Aztec's religious rituals priority with today's reasons for limiting military superiority when he states, "We do not have the sinister Tlacaxipeualiztli—Our Lord, the Flayed One—but rather the concepts of 'humanitarianism' and 'pacifism.' Our priests are lawyers and United Nations (UN) officials, and our goal the sanctity of life, not military victory."[66] Undoubtedly, this is a key statement to help understand how and why the United States has chosen to limit its own powers during an event which, and should be, reserved as last resort, precisely because its true nature is characterized by extreme violence, indiscriminate destruction, and the intended loss of life; as described by Alach:

---

[62] Ibid, 501.

[63] Ibid, 499.

[64] Ibid, 500.

[65] Zhivan Alach, "The New Aztecs: Ritual and Restraint in Contemporary Western Military Operations," last modified July 2011, 1, PDF.

[66] Ibid, 2.

The total war impulse seemingly reached its culmination in 1945. Since that critical inflection point, there has been a shift back toward ritual and restraint. This new trend is marked by a growing intolerance for casualties, both friendly and enemy, both soldier and civilian, and an emphasis on limited means of war.[67]

An attitude towards war which has been exploited by the insurgents who, by implementing the asymmetric tactics that place non-combatants in the middle, are able to effectively balance the battlefield against more powerful nations. As explained by Dr. George Van Otten, in his article *Educating MI Professionals to Meet the Challenges of Changing Geopolitical Realities and Modern Asymmetric Warfare*, "The United States' laudable abhorrence of casualties causes many analysts to view our military strategies as predictable. This perception encourages potential enemies to practice asymmetric warfare against the international interests of the United States and against our homeland."[68] So not only is the humanization of war complicating the achievement of strategic objectives in the battlefield, it is also endangering innocent civilians throughout the spectrum of the conflict.

According to Herfried Munkler, the days of symmetry in global military power when the fear of mutual annihilation forced the sides to negotiate with each other and created sides where only nation-states were engaged are gone; and the world is now fighting wars against weaker enemies who understand the disproportion of military power and have learnt to adapt and use it in a way which places the stronger nation in a lose-lose situation.[69] Munkler goes on to explain how, for America, the cases of Vietnam, Beirut, and Somalia showed the rest of the world, including a terrorist called Osama bin Laden, the greatest superpower could be defeated regardless of its military superiority.[70]

Munkler, a proponent of new wars concept, also explains how today's conflicts are more complex than before because they are characterized by an increase of non-combatants being killed and/or displaced, by an enemy that cannot be clearly identified, and a battlefield without defined lines.[71] And although Munkler makes sense in his description of today's consequences in war-torn nations, it is important to clarify here that the innate characteristics of war should be considered the same throughout history and most likely in the future

---

[67] Ibid, 13.

[68] George A. Van Otten, "Educating MI Professionals to Meet the Challenges of Changing Geopolitical Realities and Modern Asymmetric Warfare," last modified July 2002, 34, PDF.

[69] Herfried Munkler, The New Wars (Oxford: Polity, 2005), 25.

[70] Ibid, 26.

[71] Ibid, 14-15.

As explained by Antulio Echevarria, "We would, in fact, be hard pressed to find a conventional conflict in history in which the belligerents did not have as one of their chief aims the changing, if not the complete undermining, of their adversary's political will."[72] Echevarria also brings to light the fact that attacking civilians in order to influence the opponent's will is not new and that in some cases proved effective.[73] Obviously war has many characteristics that are responsible for nations not willing to conduct conventional methods of warfighting; the loss of civilian lives being the main one; however, these fears have enabled the insurgents to use populated areas as sanctuaries that stronger nations will not dare to attack. A limitation compounded by today's media availability to the battlefields.

Today's warzones are more accessible to public opinion because the images are available everywhere and in real time. The images of death and destruction are usually better exploited by the insurgency who effectively sells the picture as being victims of the world's super powers that are truly and solely responsible for the indiscriminate killing of women and children. Also, the media's dedication to show the effects the war is having on the innocent population tends to demonize the invading force; as explained by Munkler, "In any event, the use of images of war as a method of war – the transformation of war reporting into a reporting war – represents a huge step in the asymmetrization of war."[74]

By bringing the war to America's TV sets and laptops, the insurgency has effectively contaminated the political will to continue to fight; and according to Echevarria, the consensus is that will is the most important part of sustaining a war.[75] And the strategy or tactic of exploiting media has proven effective for the insurgency who understands America's weakness for casualties and who is also aware of how public opinion in the United Sates is so powerful it can go as far as to drive strategy. For example, Bing West provides a perfect description of how the media served as a tool against the American forces during Operation Vigilant Resolve against Fallujah in April of 2004:

> A Sunni cleric featured in Al Jazeera screamed, "They are killing children! They are trying to destroy everything!" Not to be outdone, the president of the Iraqi Governing Council repeated the charge that the Americans had changed from "an army of liberation" to "an army of occupation."[76]

---

[72] Antulio J. Echevarria, "Fourth-Generation War and Other Myths," last modified November 2005, 11. PDF
[73] Ibid, 11.
[74] Herfried Munkler, The New Wars (Oxford: Polity, 2005), 28.
[75] Antulio J. Echevarria, "Fourth-Generation War and Other Myths," last modified November 2005, 12. PDF

These images effectively froze the policymakers in Washington who were incapable of making the tough decision of allowing the Marines to do what they felt were sent there to do, and take total control of a city which had become a safe haven of the insurgency; creating a standoff which eventually lead to the humiliating American retreat and turning over control of the city to the same insurgency they have fought so hard against just a few days earlier.[77] Once again the civilian masters in Washington D.C. have diligently fought in a just manner and avoided further death and destruction which they believed could be replaced by building schools and hospitals.

So, has war really changed? The answer is most definitely not. The nature of war has been and always will be the same; as explained by Bart Schuurman, "Wars can therefore take on a multitude of forms, but all are shaped by the interaction between the eternal elements of violence, chance, and rational purpose."[78] And even though the new wars scholars and theorists intend to undermine the need of Clausewitz for wars today, it is undeniable that Clausewitz' trinity of war is very much alive and easily identified in every conflict. Schuurman also goes on to explain, "While the new wars theorists have made important contributions to the study of contemporary armed conflict, they also have been the cause of considerable confusion regarding fundamental aspects of war."[79]

Therefore, it should be concluded that war has not changed, what has changed is the way powers like the United States choose to approach them; and the embraced suggestion that wars today are different than any other is unfortunately having a detrimental effect over how they could be effectively fought.

---

[76] Bing West, No True Glory: A Frontline Account of the Battle for Fallujah, paperback ed. (New York: Bantam Books, 2006), 209.

[77] Ibid, 208-220.

[78] Bart Schuurman, "Clausewitz and the 'New Wars' Scholars," Parameters, Spring 2010, 94.

[79] Ibid.

5 THE UNJUSTNESS OF THE JUST PRINCIPLES

On the issue of war ethics and the law of war, Christopher Coker, a professor of International Relations at the London School of Economics, provides a functional introduction in his book *Ethics and War in the 21st Century*, where he explains the morality of wars is divided in three behaviors: the first being those who believe and promote the idea that war cannot be justified under any reason (the pacifist); the second school of thought are those who conversely believe all wars have some sort of justification (the realist); and the third group is the Just War theorists, which Coker believes the world is following today, where the justification for war may only be approved based on humanitarian reasons alone.[80]

One of the most influential figures on the Just War Theory is Michael Walzer. And while he makes outstanding contributions to humanizing wars, in his own works one can find the source of where and when the American obsession with winning hearts and minds instead of winning wars originated from. Walzer describes in detail how, after decades of being ignored, the Just War Theory was awaken in the anti-war camps during the Vietnam War; influenced by the left, they unknowingly began using the same just war terminology which is found throughout the laws governing wars today.[81]

The different aspects of the Just War Theory did not only stay with anti-war movements, it was adopted by those with greater access to the minds of future generations, the philosophers, university professors, and most worryingly of all...the military itself.[82] Walzer admits in his work that these

---

[80] Christopher Coker, Ethics and War in the 21st Century (London: Routledge, 2008), 7.
[81] Michael Walzer, "The Triumph of Just War Theory (and the Dangers of Success)," Social Research 69, no. 4 (Winter 2002): 928-929.
[82] Ibid, 929.

new teachings were not only a guide for fighting wars in a more humane manner, but they were pretty much an extension of the anti-war movement which was only based on the most unpopular war the United States had fought up to that moment.[83]

Walzer also provides an explanation of the language used to transform the approach to war and successfully constrain the US military from using its full force:

> But there was another feature of Vietnam than gave the moral critique of the war special force: it was a war that we lost, and the brutality with which we fought the war almost certainly contributed to our defeat. In a war for "hearts and minds," rather than for land and resources, justice turns out to be a key to victory.[84]

It is undeniable that this mindset is prevalent in most government officials and military leaders who have most likely been influenced by their mentors and professors throughout their military and/or academic formation; and the proof of this rests exclusively on their decision making; which is once again proudly depicted by Just War Theory champion Michael Walzer when he describes the limits drawn during the Gulf War and how the military itself started to adopt the Just War Theory language during their campaigns in Kosovo and Afghanistan; semantics that were uncommon if coming from the military; as described by Walzer, "…they commonly came from outside the armed forces – from clerics, lawyers, and professors, not from generals…"[85]

Therefore, through the attractive language of the Just War Theory and the legislative pressures originating from the laws of war, they appear to have had major success on softening the U.S. military and specially their civilian masters. Because these ideologies had a direct impact on how the United States has decided to approach its different military alternatives after WWII, it is important to explore the effects these theories and laws had over the American approach to the war in Iraq.

The Law of War Deskbook published by the International and Operational Law Department of The Judge Advocate General's Legal Center and School (TJAGLCS), which is responsible for educating and training the Army's Judge Advocate Officer Graduate and Basic Courses and the Operational Law of War Course clearly describes the law of war as originating from the Just War Theory and being divided into two main areas, Jus ad Bellum and Jus in Bello.[86]

---

[83] Ibid, 930.
[84] Ibid.
[85] Ibid, 932
[86] Jeff A. Bovarnick et al., *The Law of War Deskbook* (Charlottesville, VA: International

Additionally, the Deskbook also explains how the Law of War became officially codified by the different treaties implemented throughout history, subsequently forming two major categories these agreements fall into, The Hague Tradition and the Geneva Tradition.[87] Because many of these rules and regulations have a lasting congruency with the devastating nature of war, this research will mainly focus on those which are not only incongruent with the insurgents' tactics, but are also harming the innocent people these laws were intended to protect.

Jus ad Bellum, which the Law of War Deskbook defines as, "...the law dealing with conflict management, and how States initiate armed conflict (i.e., under what circumstances the use of military power is legally and morally justified)."[88] Is regulated by the United Nations (UN) and, in short, it is responsible for preventing nation states from using force against each other, with exception of use of force approved by the UN Security Council and actions that are originated from self-defense.[89]

Within this principle, the Deskbook also highlights the UN's concept of non-intervention, attempting to defend and protect state sovereignty,[90] apparently even above humanity itself. And while the Deskbook does make mention of humanitarian intervention, it only refers to it as nothing more than a concept and not a law which actually forces nations to protect the life and dignity of people. Although this law seems to, for the most part, have been effective among states in the international arena, it is failing to protect people internally because the laws prevent nations which stand for humanity and freedom to be able to intervene when they should; and it is precisely in this arena where most violations are being committed. A point in which Brian Orend poses an excellent question when he wrote:

> Why privilege the governance of the nation-state...if the nation-state does not deserve it? *The only way it deserves it is by earning it through its respect for, and empowerment of, the human rights of its own citizens and those of others.* States like this truly do have a moral value and are worth enabling and protecting.[91]

While Orend is an enthusiast of the Just War Theory, he is a critic of the laws governing armed conflict because they are conveniently created by the states themselves and sometimes their priorities might not be the most

---

and Operational Law Department of The Judge Advocate General's Legal Center and School, 2011), 10.

[87] Ibid, 19.

[88] Ibid, 10

[89] Ibid, 33-34.

[90] Ibid, 32.

[91] Brian Orend, *The Morality of War* (Peterborough, Ont.: Broadview Press, 2006), 37.

morally acceptable.[92] Actually, in many cases the oppressive type states are the ones benefiting from being able to cast a vote on these issues because the results end up serving as a protective blanket for these regimes to violate with impunity their people's unalienable rights; and as Orend points out, "…a rights violator is a rights violator. A group engaging in domestic rights-violation will not hesitate, if it can and if it wants, to violate rights internationally."[93] And although this is an unfortunate reality which has been proven historically, in recent times, and at this very moment, it appears the international community refuses to use history as a justifying guide to waive a government's sovereignty rights in order to defend human rights and prevent the expansion of the problem in a timely manner.

Just War theorists like Brian Orend and Michael Walzer defend the use of armed humanitarian intervention only when the circumstances have become genocidal, and use the cases of Cambodia (mid-1970s) and Kosovo (1990s) as examples of Jus ad Bellum in the name of humanity.[94] However, they also criticize the international community's hypocrisy when it picks and chooses where it should intervene for the good of humanity; as described by Orend, "Consider as Walzer says, that in recent history those countries which have cried out for armed humanitarian intervention – Somalia, Bosnia, Rwanda, Kosovo – haven't exactly been prime pieces of global real estate."[95]

In the case of the invasion of Iraq in 2003, the humanitarian case could have been argued because Saddam Hussein was a ruthless dictator after all, but why Iraq and not the rest of the nations where they are submitted to the same types of regimes or worse? As explained by Orend, everyone knew Operation Iraqi Freedom (OIF) was actually a preemptive campaign in search of WMD which could be considered one battle in the war on terror and under the argument of self-defense.[96] Therefore, as unpopular as it was, the United States had its justification for going to war against Iraq and did not have the need to make up a humanitarian case. It could be construed then, if the American approach in Iraq would have always been to topple and take control over an unruly government and not the delivery of freedom and democracy, the United States, would have spared itself from senseless stalemates, like the one in Fallujah in 2004 explained earlier, and of viewing COIN as the only humane solution to a war they were not willing to fight.

The U.S. military has done an outstanding job training their young men and women, and except for a few cases, they have developed generations of

---

[92] Ibid, 36.
[93] Ibid, 53-54.
[94] Ibid, 91.
[95] Ibid, 92.
[96] Ibid, 96.

great Americans who have represented their country proudly and with the honor and humanity of a just warrior; however, today's soldiers are sent to win their nation's wars not only under the pressure of fighting the enemy, but also by the constraints created by the rules and laws which force the soldiers to add an additional layer to their thought-process during combat.

Once in war, the U.S. military is governed by the principles found in Jus in Bello, defined by the Law of War Deskbook as, "...the law governing the actions of States once conflict has started (i.e., what legal and moral restraints apply to the conduct of waging war)."[97] Under this law are the main contributors to humanizing warfare which have successfully transformed how powers such as the United States fight their wars. While some of these principles, such as the ones covered throughout the hors de combat, are irrefutably legitimate and at par with the nature of war; there are others which are simply unattainable in any war, but even more against the style of warfare being implemented by insurgents today.

For example, the Law of War Deskbook describes Jus in Bello consisting of the principles of discrimination and proportionality;[98] two principles strictly enforced by the U.S. military during their pre-deployment classes and found in any doctrinal publication involving the use of force, such as Joint Publication (JP) 3-60 *Joint Targeting* where the appendix dedicated to the legal considerations commanders must be aware of when selecting an area to be attacked. And although this section does encourage the application of these two principles for the protection of innocent lives, it also provides flexibility to the commander to waive these codes in cases where the enemy is using noncombatants as human shields, as long as the targets are considered to be of military value.[99] Conversely, Generals Petraeus' FM 3-24 has a much more restrictive approach.

The Counterinsurgency Filed Manual is clearly focused on the protection of the noncombatant and their property at all costs, even if this results in the survival of the insurgency. The language utilized to explain discrimination and proportionality clearly encourages the American commanders to use restraint for the good of the overall strategy.[100] And where it does allow the use of force it still highlights restrictions backed by the law of war which place the forces on the ground in a conundrum of choosing between surviving or facing a jury; for example FM 3-24 states,

---

[97] Jeff A. Bovarnick et al., *The Law of War Deskbook* (Charlottesville, VA: International and Operational Law Department of The Judge Advocate General's Legal Center and School, 2011), 10.

[98] Ibid, 13-14.

[99] Joint Chiefs of Staff, *Joint Publication 3-60: Joint Targeting* (n.p.: n.p., 2007), E-2.

[100] David H. Petraeus and James F. Amos, *The United States Army and the United States Marine Corps Counterinsurgency Field Manual* (Kissimmee, FL: Signalman Publishing, 2006), 7-7.

"Soldiers and Marines must take all feasible precautions when choosing means and methods of attack to avoid and minimize loss of civilian life, injury to civilians, and damage to civilian objects."[101]

Unlike JP 3-60 which leaves open an option to attack a legal target when deemed necessary, FM 3-24 does not. And even though it could be argued that JP 3-60 is mostly applicable for fighting a conventional enemy, and COIN is a total different environment requiring alternative tactics to minimize the amount of collateral damage created by U.S. forces, then it must be contended that American soldiers are being trained the basics of warfighting in one way and ordered to fight in a much different one. A puzzling approach due to the fact that the enemy the United States has been fighting for the past decade is an insurgency and because America's overwhelming military power will continue to maintain the mismatched characteristic of asymmetric warfare.

Dr. Goldstein, an associate professor of political science at California State University, argues in her article titled *Just War Theory and Democratization by Force* that the failure of the United States in Iraq and Afghanistan was not the special cultural and economic factors of these countries compared to Germany and Japan after WWII, but rather it was because the United States failed to break the will of the locals to continue to fight before engaging in its nation-building efforts.[102] Also, Goldstein explains how total victory is unachievable if a military is constrained by Jus in Bello and if it follows the concept of limited war; and if total victory is not achieved, then neither will democratization by force.[103] America's choice of restraint and the minimization of the use of force as much as possible are described by Dr. Cora Sol Goldstein:

> The United States exerted restraint in fighting the wars in Afghanistan and Iraq to minimize collateral damage. Both the Bush and the Obama administrations adhered to the modern standards of lawfare. While the U.S. Air Force used 5,000-pound, laserguided bomb units (GBU-28) to target cave and tunnel complexes in southern Afghanistan, the Bush administration refrained from using tactical nuclear weapons against Al-Qaeda. The nuclear version of the GBU-28, the B61-11, was not used. Similarly the Obama administration rejected the proposal of an airstrike by B-2 Spirit bombers to destroy bin Laden's residential compound, because launching 32 2,000-pound smart bombs would have destroyed the entire city of Abbottabad. In order to minimize civilian casualties, both Bush and Obama embraced the use of small units of special

---

[101] Ibid.

[102] Cora Sol Goldstein, "Just War Theory and Democratization by Force," *Military Review*, September/October 2012, 2-3.

[103] Ibid, 3.

operations forces as well as smart weapons to launch precision strikes against military targets.[104]

This is simply another example of the law of war and ideologies such as the Just War Theory are winning the war for the insurgents and are effectively dismantling America's military superiority. It also demonstrates how the American leadership is not really committed to achieving victory and is more interested in managing public opinion as a strategy for dealing with today's enemy.

Unfortunately, the concept of victory in COIN has nothing to do with defeating the enemy; as explained in the FM 3-24, "Victory is achieved when the populace consents to the government's legitimacy and stops actively and passively supporting the insurgency."[105] A very different philosophy from the generals responsible for winning America's wars in the past; for instance, Jeffrey Record quoted the great General MacArthur as stating in front of congress, "Once war is forced upon us, there is no other alternative than to apply every available means to bring it to a swift end. War's very object is victory, not prolonged indecision. In war there is no substitute for victory."[106]

And it is precisely prolonged indecision what the laws of war, as they are currently established, are creating. In fact, in an effort to maintain the legitimacy of the Just War Theory, Michael Walzer in his article titled *Coda: Can the Good Guys Win?* creates a series of arguments which should be considered because of today's style of warfare being imposed by the insurgency and clearly supports the intent of this research. Today's complicated environment has created a duality in war that is best explained in Walzer's own words:

> In what is called 'asymmetric warfare', between states and non-state actors, between high-tech military organizations and low-tech insurgent forces, the insurgents argue that it is not possible for them to win unless they hide among their own civilians and launch terror attacks against the enemy's civilians. And their enemies claim that it is not possible to respond effectively to these attacks without inflicting harm on the civilian population within which the insurgents are hiding – harm that exceeds what is permitted by the standards (as they are understood today) of *jus in bello* and of international law.[107]

---

[104] Ibid, 7.
[105] David H. Petraeus and James F. Amos, *The United States Army and the United States Marine Corps Counterinsurgency Field Manual* (Kissimmee, FL: Signalman Publishing, 2006), 1-3.
[106] Jeffrey Record, *Beating Goliath: Why Insurgencies Win* (Washington, DC: Potomac Books, 2007), 108.

It is obvious today that the insurgencies have adopted the use of innocent civilians as their best form of protection against the stronger forces who are strictly governed by the laws of war which prevents them from targeting civilian areas, especially if COIN is the presiding strategy.

Because the laws of armed conflict are being interpreted so strictly by American politicians and generals, and the real-time media reporting taking place in every conflict around the globe, it has become impossible to fight insurgencies with the amount of violence and destruction which would deny them of any safe haven, avoid a protracted conflict, and seek the insurgencies annihilation to avoid a future resurgence; as explained by Walzer, "It seems to follow, then, that terrorism is immoral, and fighting against the terrorists is not morally possible."[108]

However, Walzer strongly believes that the best way to defeat this new type of enemy is to fight justly and to use constraint as the best tool to fight this war, and he explains how America's military leadership is thinking in the same way; as he stated, "In any case, it is clear that leading military figures believe that it is possible to win within the constraints of *jus in bello* – and even that it is not possible to win outside those constraints."[109] And because the pacifist are winning the war on war, it has made COIN the most attractive approach for stronger nations like the United States in order to paint a more humanitarian image, avoid casualties on either side, and most importantly satisfy the public opinion.

Meanwhile, American soldiers are required to risk their lives by fighting with the constraints imposed by their leadership; as described by Major Lance Boothe, an Army Artillery Officer and veteran of both Iraq and Afghanistan who served as the Army's chief of Field Artillery Concepts Development Division in the Capabilities Development and Integration Directorate, Fires Center of Excellence, "…rules of engagement complicates matters. Most tactical commanders are not willing to use quick-fire procedures that make counterfire effective. Nor will most tactical commanders doing COIN accept the collateral damage that may result from shooting quickly with area munitions."[110]

In his article, *King No More*, Major Boothe also delivers chilling anecdotes where due to the ROEs American servicemen are being killed because they are denied the readily available fire support they are so effectively trained to use.[111] Adding to this list of witnesses is Bing West's

---

[107] Michael Walzer, "Coda: Can the Good Guys Win?," *The European Journal of International Law* 24, no. 1 (2013): 433-434.

[108] Ibid, 436.

[109] Ibid, 443-444.

[110] Lance Boothe, "King No More," *Military Review*, May/June 2013, 75.

[111] Ibid, 74.

book *No true Glory*, where he provides a vivid narrative of a Cobra pilot refusing to support a Marine platoon because the fear of violating the ROEs, even with the assurance of no friendlies in the area, the company commander is required to send in his Marines and risk their lives to eliminate a target which should have been considered legal.[112]

Noticeably, the ROEs required to support COIN operations have detrimental effects over the morale of the men and women serving in the combat zones where this strategy is being implemented. For example, in the article *Rules of Engagement and Abusive Citizens* by Amitai Etzioni, a Professor of International Affairs and Director of the Institute for Communitarian Policy Studies at George Washington University, it explains, "Reducing civilian casualties is considered a key element of this strategy. Such restraint was urged even if it came at the expense of the military's ability to operate."[113]

A risky decision which not only affects the soldier's mindset but also places them in physical danger by allowing the battlefield to be leveled or in favor of the insurgency; as described by Etzioni, "...the unit came under attack by small arms fire and rocket-propelled grenades and requested artillery support, which was denied due to fear of collateral damage and concern for civilian structures."[114] Unfortunately, these are some of the demoralizing realities American troops under a COIN strategy have to face when dealing with an enemy that does not care for loss of life on either side. This is not to say COIN does not have utility within military doctrine or as part of a campaign, but the idea of COIN as a strategy to win wars, especially in a country like Iraq, certainly must be challenged.

So at this point it is safe to state that the laws of war are inherently unjust for the stronger side and unjustly beneficial for the insurgency which uses them as their best available defense apparatus, but what about the ones in the middle of the conflict the laws of war are meant to protect? Has COIN, a strategy based on the protection of the civilian bystanders, achieved its main objective of providing the people a stable local government able to govern with legitimacy?

In the case of Iraq there are many who view General Petraeus as the savior of a war that was reawakening memories of Vietnam. For example, in 2012, Bing West, who has witnessed firsthand the wars in Iraq and Afghanistan, affirmed in his book *The Wrong War* that General Petraeus was directly responsible for the improvement of the Iraq War[115] and presented

---

[112] Bing West, *No True Glory: A Frontline Account of the Battle for Fallujah*, paperback ed. (New York: Bantam Books, 2006), 343.
[113] Amitai Etzioni, "Rules of Engagement and Abusive Citizens," PRISM 4, no. 4 (2014): 89.
[114] Ibid, 90.
[115] Francis J. West, *The Wrong War: Grit, Strategy, and the Way out of Afghanistan*, random house trade paperback ed. (New York: Random House Trade Paperbacks, 2012),

the arrival of Petraeus in Afghanistan as the best thing that could have happened because of his success in Iraq.[116] Nevertheless, apart from the COIN detractors covered earlier, the best measure of success or failure in Iraq is the current situation in this country.

Once President Obama fulfilled his promise of pulling every combat unit out of Iraq by 2010, the reality of the effects of the COIN strategy started to come into light. As prophesized by Pollack and Sargsyan, the political situation in Iraq started to crumble immediately after the U.S. military departure and the organizations meant to protect the people could not be trusted; as explained by Anthony Cordesman in his 2014 article *Iraq: A Time to Act*:

> Maliki has also steadily corrupted and polarized the Iraqi security forces and central government since coming back into power following the 2010 election, and there are serious limits to what Special Forces and other U.S. advisers can do without taking sides in the renewed civil war that Maliki has provoked.[117]

Just four years after the American withdrawal the security situation in Iraq has turned into a regional humanitarian disaster. According to the United Nations High Commissioner for Refugees (UNHCR) 2013 started to see a new wave of internally displaced personnel and by the first quarter of 2014 the number of displaced was well over 427,000.[118] The vacuum created by the departure of U.S. forces allowed for the resurgence of a stronger and more ruthless insurgency under the banner of the Islamic State. The current political, security, and humanitarian reality in Iraq are all good evidence that COIN in Iraq failed to achieve the strategic objectives required to bring a true lasting stable environment where civilians can thrive. Retired Army Colonel Andrew Bacevich in his book *Breach of Trust* makes a valid point on what has become the reality of COIN in Iraq:

> Petraeus offered deliverance of a sort – he "exemplified the Army finally getting it right in Iraq," one officer observed – thereby facilitating its escape from Golgotha. Yet COIN could not provide a lasting remedy for the collapse of institutional purpose in Iraq. For the best army in the world, "getting it right" was not the same as winning.[119]

173.
[116] Ibid, 225.
[117] Anthony H. Cordesman, "Iraq: A Time to Act," CSIS, last modified August 6, 2014, accessed October 4, 2014.
[118] United Nations High Commissioner for Refugees, comp., *UNHCR Iraq Fact Sheet* (n.p.: n.p., 2014), 1-2.
[119] Andrew J. Bacevich, *Breach of Trust: How Americans Failed Their Soldiers and*

COIN simply became the convenient way of fighting wars because, as explained by Colonel Gian Gentile, its language provides politicians with a moral coziness of a war filled with humanitarian objectives that is easier to sell to the public, but one which at the end has always led to failure.[120] In the case of Iraq, COIN appears to have worked as an exit tool that allowed the United States to get out and hope for the best; and the best simply did not happen, especially for the sector which COIN and the laws of war so hardly intended to protect, the Iraqi people. The current events taking place in Iraq and Syria and that are now starting to directly affect NATO ally Turkey is unfortunately the best evidence of America's failure in the Iraq War.

While America chose to carry out a limited campaign and conduct a strategy as humane as COIN to fight a ruthless enemy with no regards for humanity at all, not even for their own people; there are clear indications this new insurgency will end up using the same tactics that so effectively constrained the United States and its allies...discrimination and proportionality; a lethal combination that is defeating the most advanced war technology and strongest militaries in the world. As witnessed by the soldiers who fought in Iraq and expressed in the book *Nightcap at Dawn: American Soldiers' Counterinsurgency in Iraq* by J.B. Walker, the insurgents would simply hide within the civilian population leaving the Americans without options but to walk away, even when they knew who they were and where they were.[121]

Now, as the United States and its new coalition announced their plans to attack Islamic State of Iraq and the Levant (ISIL) targets in Iraq and Syria, the insurgents once again are preparing to use proportionality and discrimination in their favor; as reported by Daniel Wiser of the Washington Free Beacon, "President Barack Obama has missed a key opportunity to deliver a blow to Islamic militants in Iraq by authorizing only limited airstrikes... Now the jihadists are blending in with the civilian population, making them much more difficult to target."[122]

In the meantime, while the international community refuses to use real force for the good of humanity and respect for sovereignty, it cowardly

---

Their Country (New York: Metropolitan Books, Henry Holt and Company, 2013), 108.

[120] Gian P. Gentile, *Wrong Turn: America's Deadly Embrace of Counterinsurgency* (New York: New Press, 2013), 139-140.

[121] J. B. Walker, *Nightcap at Dawn: American Soldiers' Counterinsurgency in Iraq* (New York: Skyhorse Pub., 2012), 372-380.

[122] Daniel Wiser, "Limited U.S. Airstrikes in Iraq Impede Fight against ISIL," The Washington Free Beacon, last modified August 14, 2014, accessed October 5, 2014, http://freebeacon.com/national-security/limited-u-s-airstrikes-in-iraq-impede-fight-against-isil/.

watches how ISIL brutally commits a myriad of crimes against humanity and deliberately violates every law of war; as described by the Human Rights Office and the UN in their *Report on the Protection of Civilians in Armed Conflict in Iraq: 6 July – 10 September 2014*:

> According to information corroborated by different sources, ISIL and associated armed groups carried out attacks deliberately and systematically targeting civilians and civilian infrastructure, with the intention of killing and wounding civilians. ISIL and associated armed groups also continued to systematically perpetrate targeted assassinations and abductions, including community, political, and religious leaders, government employees, education professionals, journalists, and health workers.[123]

Additionally, this same report accounts for at least of 24,015 civilians killed or injured, almost 1.8 million people displaced, massive executions carried out against the ISF, rapes of women and children, destruction of property and religious/cultural infrastructure, and the denial of inherent human rights.[124] The numbers and acts described in this report are eye-opening and, unfortunately, undeniable consequences of the United States sparing so many insurgents' lives during their hearts and minds campaign just a few years earlier and their distinct impatience that is ironically incompatible with COIN.

Also, the misery and unjustness being carried out against these innocent and defenseless civilians is being protracted by the refusal of the international community to use a sizeable force that can finally not only put an end to these lawless individuals, but also to send a message to the rest of the terrorist world that they will not be allowed safe haven ever again, even if that cost includes the unavoidable tragedy of collateral damages and deaths. However, it appears the United States will once again opt for one of the many forms of warfare it has designed to restrain its own military might; as it could be interpreted from the U.S. Secretary of State, John Kerry, who refuses to call the situation against ISIL as war and instead refers to it as an antiterrorism action, while the Obama administration assured ISIL it will not have to face American troops in their newly establish Islamic State.[125] These are unfortunately clear indications that the United States will continue to reject history as a guideline for the future and the lessons from

---

123 UNAMI/OHCHR, *Report on the Protection of Civilians in Armed Conflict in Iraq: 6 July – 10 September 2014* (n.p.: n.p., 2014), 5.

124 Ibid, i.

125 Elise Labott, Laura Smith-Spark, and Ray Sanchez, "Kerry: U.S. not at war with ISIS," CNN, last modified September 11, 2014, accessed October 5, 2014, http://www.cnn.com/2014/09/11/world/meast/kerry-mideast-visit-isis/index.html.

the long list of failed campaigns will be revisited in a near future.

6 CONCLUSIONS AND FINDINGS

This research explored the implementation of COIN in Iraq and its most observable outcome to date; it also analyzed the reason for using these types of operations as an alternative for war; and it created a link between the laws of war, as they are today, and COIN being the best alternative for political and military leaders to adhere to these rules. The investigation conducted for this thesis found multiple factors indicating a transformation in the American mindset which prevents it from waging war as it did in WWII and it is probably the main reason for having difficulty winning wars thereafter, even against much weaker enemies.

The most noticeable impact over America's warfighting capabilities has been the constraints imposed on the U.S. military from being able to implement its full capacity when going into war. Yes, even on a limited basis the U.S. military is able to defeat a conventional army and topple governments in record time; however, the United States is failing to connect its military objectives with its political ones, which is the main reason why nations go to war in the first place. The two main aspects of the laws of war, proportionality and discrimination, have made it morally impossible for the United States to destroy an insurgency through military means; which has forced the United States to renounce to its conventional warfighting methods, leading to protracted conflicts where the will of the American people and the policymakers who ironically started the event start to dwindle and the idea of success, also known as victory, are no longer a priority.

Most troublesome is the fact that the U.S. military leadership has bought into the ideology of placing their soldiers in the same level of care as the local population of the occupied nation; a method resented by the men and women who are in the frontlines witnessing firsthand the unjustness of this system. The constraints imposed on the American warfighter has generated a dangerous indecisiveness that was clearly projected in Fallujah where the United States had the opportunity to eliminate the problem, but instead allowed it to metastasize because the potential for high casualty rates was too high, a clear indication that the American mentality is no longer compatible with the realities of the nature of warfare.

The research found that it is undeniably true that the rules of war are actually aiding insurgencies to level the battlefield. The insurgents purposely use populated areas to prevent stronger nations like the United States from being able to use weapons that can cause greater area damage, and in the case of Fallujah the insurgents learnt how hesitant the American leadership will be to send in ground forces where high casualty rates may occur on any side of the battle. Once again proportionality and discrimination are vital in the way today wars are being fought, and this research highlights the fact of how the insurgents actually use the key principles of Jus in Bello to level the battlefield and in many cases tip it to their favor.

This thesis also demonstrated the demoralizing effects these rules have over American troops who not only feel like there are fighting with their hands behind their back, but how there is a sense of abandonment from those who put them in harm's way in the first place. Additionally, through the testimonials of the soldiers who have had to actually operate under the ROEs imposed to them for the good of the COIN strategy, this research was able to discover the sense of frustration and impotence American servicemen had to work through during their deployments to Iraq. These are all clear indicators that the laws of war do have a direct impact on the battlefield which works towards the insurgency's favor, allowing them to prolong the conflict enough for the American political and public will to fight to be weaken; however, although the research did find demoralizing effects over the American troops, it did not find any evidence that their will to fight was ever diminished.

What this research was able to discover, nevertheless, is that the fundamental problem with America's new approach to war is that there has been for years now, a wave of theorists who have been trying to change the concept of war and apparently they have been fairly successful as it can be evidenced by America's approach to war after WWII. With many of these experts promoting the idea that the teachings of Clausewitz are irrelevant for the modern war, the United States has resorted to winning the hearts and minds instead of winning wars. It seems as if the American leadership strongly believes that wars can and should be humanized, and because they are trying to do so, the United States is failing to achieve overwhelming and timely victory.

An essential effect the alternate way which the United States is approaching war against insurgencies is that leadership sees themselves in a no-win situation where too much force will produce negative effects and too little will not produce anything; therefore, they decided to design new forms of warfare where they are attempting to please the international rules of war and most importantly the public opinion. Unfortunately, the United States is in a dangerous state of denial that these amorphous forms of warfare are really not achieving America's strategic objectives and are instead creating new post-Vietnam sentiments of failure with the same psychological effects that will prevent America from using its mighty military the way it should.

And even though the best way to judge the true outcome of a war or a strategy implemented for it is hindsight, in the case of Iraq it was not necessary to allow decades to pass in order to see that the effects of COIN in Iraq failed to produce the desired outcome. Unfortunately, because of America's telegraphed departure from Iraq, this research had difficulty establishing if the reduction of violence was truly due to the effects of COIN in the region or if it was because the insurgency were smart enough to wait for the withdraw of the American troops. Nevertheless, by seeing the conditions Iraq is in today, just four years after the United States left, it is clear that the strategy implemented during the Iraq War failed to produce a long-lasting stability characteristic of a successful campaign.

Current events show the ease with which ISIL is plowing through the ISF and controlling entire cities like Fallujah where even the United States had a much more difficult time to take over. What this proves is that COIN failed to adequately train the forces responsible for maintaining the security and stability of Iraq. Also, it might be the clearest indication that the insurgency did go quiet while the United States left nothing behind and as soon as the terrorists were presented with the right time, they simply came out of their training camps stronger, faster, and better equipped than ever before. And, by failing to achieve the total destruction of the insurgency, the United States is directly responsible for the regional turmoil taking place today which has created a humanitarian disaster with millions being displaced, thousands being murdered, and cultures being exterminated by an insurgency with no regards for humanity whatsoever. Now, while the United States tries to hold on to the moral high-ground, the insurgents are effectively holding on to the tactical and strategic one.

On the question, are the rules of war causing more harm than good in today's conflicts, this research concluded that undeniably there is a use and a need for laws and regulations to govern why countries fight wars and how their soldiers act during their battles. It is critical not to allow innocent civilians to be purposely targeted by any side of the spectrum as it was done in past conflicts like WWII; and it is just as important that the soldiers involved in the conflict do not lose their human instincts and instead fight their battles with honor and dignity characteristic of a civilized world;

nevertheless, this research found tremendous incongruences these rules create with today's insurgencies. If law abiding nations try to fight by these rules, they will most likely be embarking onto a road to failure due to the fact that insurgencies are using the rules to their favor by fighting under a protective layer, ironically created by their stronger enemies.

The consequences derived from the laws of war and the persistent efforts of countries like the United States to follow them with rigidity was exemplified in Iraq where a clear victory was never achieved. The intentions of the United States to fight strictly by the rules and implement a strategy where casualty rates are low, allowed for many of the insurgents to be spared alongside the innocent civilians they would later victimize anyway.

By choosing COIN as their strategy, the American decision-makers also allowed for the conflict to extend past the American patience and support for the war, which lead to the political urgency to leave Iraq before the work of COIN was ever completed. Undoubtedly, the laws of war and specially, the way America's leadership interpreted them and applied them in Iraq, might have saved innumerable civilian lives, but in the end, they proved unjust towards the American soldiers who were unnecessarily placed in greater danger; unjust towards the outcome of the war that eventually witnessed the new rise of an insurgency which not only looks more like a conventional army now, but it is more ruthless and barbaric than ever before; and consequentially, unjust towards the civilian population the United States fought so hardly to protect and are now living a hell on earth.

So, what must be done in order to uphold the legitimacy of the rules of war? The first and most important step that must be taken is the actual enforcement of these rules, but it must be done forcedly and the response must be immediate in order to avoid any group from committing crimes against humanity and establishing themselves throughout civilian populations that would create the scenario civilized nations want to avoid. What must be prevented at all cost, however, is that insurgencies use these civilian areas as protective bubbles where the laws of war unjustly limit the stronger nations while aiding the lawless groups. This should become in line with the American policy of never negotiating with terrorists and regardless of the collateral damages, as unfortunate as it is, the insurgents will be denied any form of safe haven. Ideally, the laws of war will be readdressed and the rules readapted to the lessons learned from Iraq where in the long-run the humanistic approach to the conflict at the time, enabled the detrimental effects witnessed in the near future.

Without a doubt, the US military is more than capable of winning wars while adhering to the rules of armed conflict. However, the United States cannot allow itself to become paralyzed and ineffective when these are unbalanced and/or exploited by their enemy. It must be very cognizant of war and avoid it by all possible means, but once it becomes unavoidable, the United States must be committed to it with the understanding that death and destruction is the nature of warfare and it is meant to be that way for the very reason of imposing its will over the enemy as quickly as possible. There will be time to demonstrate America's humanity after the last shot is fired, but it is critical to first completely eliminate the threat before attempting to reconstruct. America must implement what has worked for them in the past and stop using what has failed.

REFERENCES

Alach, Zhivan. "The New Aztecs: Ritual and Restraint in Contemporary Western Military Operations." Last modified July 2011. PDF.

Al-Qaeda's Resurgence in Iraq: A Threat to U.S. Interests: Hearings Before the Committee on Foreign Affairs (2014) (statement of Mr. Brett McGurk).

Bacevich, Andrew J. *Breach of Trust: How Americans Failed Their Soldiers and Their Country.* New York: Metropolitan Books, Henry Holt and Company, 2013.

Boothe, Lance. "King No More." *Military Review,* May/June 2013, 72-78.

Bovarnick, Jeff A., Jeremy Marsh, John B. Reese, Shane R. Reeves, Robert E. Barnsby, Andrew D. Gillman, and Iain Pedden. *The Law of War Deskbook.* Charlottesville, VA: International and Operational Law Department of The Judge Advocate General's Legal Center and School, 2011.

Coker, Christopher. *Ethics and War in the 21st Century.* London: Routledge, 2008.

Cordesman, Anthony H. "Iraq: A Time to Act." CSIS. Last modified August 6, 2014. Accessed October 4, 2014.

Cordesman, Anthony H., and Emma Davies. *Iraq's Insurgency and the Road to Civil Conflict.* Portsmouth: Greenwood Publishing Group, 2008.

Echevarria, Antulio J. "Fourth-Generation War and Other Myths." Last modified November 2005. PDF.

Gentile, Gian P. *Wrong Turn: America's Deadly Embrace of Counterinsurgency.* New York: New Press, 2013.

Goldstein, Cora Sol. "Just War Theory and Democratization by Force." *Military Review*, September/October 2012, 2-8.

Gray, Colin S. "Enemies and the Essence of Strategy: Can the American Way of War Adapt?" Last modified March 2006. PDF.

Hasim, Ahmed S. *Insurgency and Counter-Insurgency in Iraq.* Ithaca, NY: Cornell University Press, 2006.

"The Iraq-ISIS Conflict in Maps, Photos and Video." The New York Times. Last modified August 20, 2014. Accessed September 2, 2014. http://www.nytimes.com/interactive/2014/06/12/world/middleeast/the-iraq-isis-conflict-in-maps-photos-and-video.html?_r=0.

Joint Chiefs of Staff. *Joint Publication 3-60: Joint Targeting.* N.p.: n.p., 2007.

Labott, Elise, Laura Smith-Spark, and Ray Sanchez. "Kerry: U.S. not at war with ISIS." CNN. Last modified September 11, 2014. Accessed October 5, 2014. http://www.cnn.com/2014/09/11/world/meast/kerry-mideast-visit-isis/index.html.

Ledwidge, Frank. *Losing Small Wars. British Military Failure in Iraq and Afghanistan.* New Haven: Yale University Press, 2011.

Munkler, Herfried. *The New Wars.* Oxford: Polity, 2005.

Murphy, Dan. "Briefing: What is the Islamic State in Iraq and the Levant (ISIS)?" The Christian Science Monitor. Last modified June 23, 2014. Accessed September 2, 2014. http://www.csmonitor.com/World/Middle-East/2014/0623/Briefing-What-is-the-Islamic-State-In-Iraq-and-the-Levant-ISIS.

Office of the Clerk. Last modified October 10, 2002. Accessed August 29, 2014. http://clerk.house.gov/evs/2002/roll455.xml.

Orend, Brian. *The Morality of War*. Peterborough, Ont.: Broadview Press, 2006.

Petraeus, David H., and James F. Amos. *The United States Army and the United States Marine Corps Counterinsurgency Field Manual*. Kissimmee, FL: Signalman Publishing, 2006.

Pollack, Kenneth M., and Irena L. Sargsyan. "The Other Side of the COIN: Perils of Premature Evacuation from Iraq." *Washington Quarterly* 33, no. 2 (Spring 2010): 17-32. Accessed August 17, 2014. DOI:10.1080/01636601003661787.

Record, Jeffrey. *Beating Goliath: Why Insurgencies Win*. Washington, DC: Potomac Books, 2007.

Schurman, Bart. "Clausewitz and the 'New Wars' Scholars." *Parameters*, Spring 2010, 89-100.

Sullivan, Patricia L. "War Aims and War Outcomes: Why Powerful States Lose Limited Wars." *Journal of Conflict Resolution* 51, no. 3 (June 2007): 496-520.

UNAMI/OHCHR. *Report on the Protection of Civilians in Armed Conflict in Iraq: 6 July – 10 September 2014*. N.p.: n.p., 2014.

United Nations High Commissioner for Refugees, comp. *UNHCR Iraq Fact Sheet*. N.p.: n.p., 2014.

United States Senate. Last modified October 11, 2002. Accessed August 29, 2014. http://www.senate.gov/legislative/LIS/roll_call_lists/roll_call_vote_cfm.cfm?congress=107&session=2&vote=00237.

Van Otten, George A. "Educating MI Professionals to Meet the Challenges of Changing Geopolitical Realities and Modern Asymmetric Warfare." Last modified July 2002. PDF.

Walker, J. B. *Nightcap at Dawn: American Soldiers' Counterinsurgency in Iraq*. New York: Skyhorse Pub., 2012.

Walker, Lydia. "Forging a Key, Turning a Lock: Counterinsurgency Theory in Iraq 2006-2008." *Studies in Conflict & Terrorism* 32, no. 10 (October 2009): 909-18. Accessed August 17, 2014. DOI:10.1080/10576100903185586.

Walzer, Michael. "Coda: Can the Good Guys Win?" *The European Journal of International Law* 24, no. 1 (2013): 433-44.

———. "The Triumph of Just War Theory (and the Dangers of Success)." *Social Research* 69, no. 4 (Winter 2002): 925-42.

West, Bing. *No True Glory: A Frontline Account of the Battle for Fallujah.* Paperback ed. New York: Bantam Books, 2006.

———. *The Wrong War: Grit, Strategy, and the Way out of Afghanistan.* Random House Trade paperback ed. New York: Random House Trade Paperbacks, 2012.

Wiser, Daniel. "Limited U.S. Airstrikes in Iraq Impede Fight against ISIL." The Washington Free Beacon. Last modified August 14, 2014. Accessed October 5, 2014. http://freebeacon.com/national-security/limited-u-s-airstrikes-in-iraq-impede-fight-against-isil/.